NO ACTUAL BUNNIES WERE PHYSICALLY HARMED OR EMOTIONALLY DAMAGED IN THE MAKING OF THIS BOOK.

ALL OCCURRENCES OF LOVE AND HATE WERE SIMULATED BY PROFESSIONAL BUNNIES UNDER CONTROLLED CONDITIONS. FOR YOUR OWN SAFETY, <u>PLEASE DO NOT TRY THIS AT HOME.</u>

Good plan

it's happy bunny™
Love Bites

By Jim Benton

SCHOLASTIC INC.

New York   Toronto   London   Aukland   Sydney
Mexico City   New Delhi   Hong Kong   Buenos Aires

For Mary K, in whom I did find true love.
It probably won't ever happen for her,
but so what?

ISBN 0-439-69345-4

Copyright © 2005 by Jim Benton

12 11 10 9 8 7 6 5 4 3 2   5 6 7 8 9 10/0

Printed in the Singapore   40

First printing, January 2005

So you have a crush.

What are you going to
do about it?

Chapter 1
The Crush

Getting people to focus on what's most important:
YOU.

Let your new crush know that you're sincere and genuine.

Show that cutey-patootey
your smart and sensitive side.

And most important of all,
tell that lil' hottie you think
they're the best.

Quiz Time!

What's the very best gift to give your crush at this stage in the game?

A) A box of candy after you have gently kissed each and every individual chocolate.

B) A bouquet of long-stemmed roses after you have passionately embraced every flower.

C) A cute little stuffed animal that you have furiously made out with.

Answer: All of these are great answers, as long as you never lose sight of the real reason to give a gift: *To Get Something in Return.* (Also check local laws: It is illegal in several states to make out with a stuffed animal.)

yah,
that's right.

You've flirted a little,
you've coughed up a gift.
Now it's time to get
to know your
cutesy-wootsy monkeyface.

please don't ever use this.
I may have to hurt you.

Chapter 2
Spying

It's just like when two people in love go for a long walk except one of them doesn't know they're being followed.

↑

Remind you of someone?

JK

Is spying as bad
as it sounds?

C'mon.
They're in *your* thoughts.
You're in *their* bushes.
It all evens out.

And it's a good way to protect
your dumplin' from danger.

Like the danger of
meeting somebody
better than you.

And besides, isn't
spying just another
way of saying
"I luv you so much
I'm willing to
invade your privacy
to prove it"?

Quiz Time!

So now you've found your soul mate. What's the perfect next move?

A) Promise to stop spying. (And for crying out loud, try to sound like you mean it!)

BAHAHA!!!!

B) Stop calling at 3:00 in the morning. Most agree that crazy should not start much before 6:00 A.M.

← that's so me =·= I'm a creeper

C) Buy your smoochyface another gift. Everybody knows that gifts are really pretty much the exact same thing as love.

→ Again... never use.

Now that all your charm
has worked its magic,
you're ready to . . .

Chapter 3
Let the Love Flow

Always tell your
honey-bunny
how cute they are.

Show your <u>snooky-wookums</u>
that you care.

Let your buttercup know
that your feelings are deep.

that's deep
man...

Quiz Time!

What's the very best nickname to call your true love at this stage in the game?

A) Kissy-wissy-tickley tummy

B) Smoochy-woochy-boochy-koochy

C) Ootsy-bootsy-shmootsy bear

like me?!?
yah--
↑

Answer: All are great choices, but if you say more than one at a time, innocent bystanders may become sick in their own mouths.

Fun and Games!

The terrific thing about love is that so many great games have been invented as a result. Here are a few you'll enjoy whether you want to or not.

"No, You Hang Up."

Why end a call like a normal human being when you can indulge in the enjoyable sport of arguing about who should hang up first?

"Hey, Let's Fight!"

It's easy to play and even easier to win. Simply be the first to ask a question the other person won't be able to answer without causing a huge argument. Try these for starters:

Which one of us loves the other one more?

NEVER ASK ←

Do you think I'm fatter than when we met?

If we broke up, which one of my friends would you date? ↑

wouldn't that still piss you off either way around?

"What's Wrong? Nothing."

You can play for just a few minutes, hours, or even weeks on end. And the rules are so simple to learn!

Now that you're officially
going out, you
can finally enjoy . . .

Chapter 4

The Unrelenting Daily Grind of Pure Love

This is about the time
when you start to learn much
more about each other.

Maybe more than you want to learn.

And you can tell each other
exactly what you're thinking.

And you'll be able to spot
each other's subtle signals.

Quiz Time!

Okay, so things are a little shaky. What now?

A) Pretend everything is okay, and don't listen to anybody who says otherwise. (Practice this: "La la la la la I can't hear you I can't hear you la la la la la la la.") ← It works ☺

B) Ask your snuggly-wuggly if they have any friends that are as cute as they are, but, you know, *way* less irritating.

C) Gosh, I don't know. What do do people do with old stinky dogs when they start to get shaky?

Answer: This depends. If you're gross, you can't be that picky, and you might have to repair this relationship. But if you're really hot, you might be entitled to expect something better.

↑ like Emma

What more can
you say about the
love that lasts
forever?

Chapter 5
It's
Over.

Breaking up is hard.
Be gentle.

Take some responsibility.

Be flexible and mature.

Quiz Time!

What's the best way to close the door on this relationship?

A) Stick relationship's neck in car door, and close it over and over and over again.

B) Tell everyone that breaking up was all your idea. A mass e-mailing costs a lot less than years of therapy. ← I disagree. I like the sympathy 😊 and presents 😊

C) Have former sweetheart's name replaced in butt tattoo. (Don't make the same mistake again. A more sensible butt tattoo should just read: **YO, THIS IS MY BUTT!**)

Answer: Hooray! All of these are correct. You might also ask for all of your gifts back, but don't be surprised if that little stuffed animal you slobbered all over doesn't want to come back.

Bonus Fun!
The Break-up Letter

It's always better to break up in person,
but sometimes you just don't feel like it.

Why not save yourself some time and use
this letter instead? Just circle whichever
red words are most appropriate.

Letters are so much better . . . .

Dear **(insert name),**

Thanks for the several pleasant **days** **weeks** **milkshakes** that we shared. Although at first it seemed as though we were a match made in **heaven** **Cleveland** **haste**, I realize now that I need something **more** **less hairy** **not psycho** in my life.
♡

Hurting you is the **last** **first** thing I'd ever want to do, but I can't hide my **feelings** **new romance** **disgust** any longer. I hope you **understand** **heal quickly** **choke on vomit**.
♡

When you think back on what we had, I hope that you'll be **kind** **happy** **floating facedown in a river**, and you'll always
♡
know that part of me will **always** **never** care about you.

I want you to know that I shall always treasure deeply, with all my heart, the beautiful memory of when we **(pick some stupid thing you did once)**, and I will never think of it as just some stupid thing we did once.

Love, **Your Friend Always,** **Cram it,**
♡
(Sign your name)

So now that you've finally wriggled your way out of that stranglehold and you're free at last . . .

Try out the Love Maze and see where your heart leads you!

START

Take some time off to enjoy being single.

Focus on some of your other interests or hobbies.

Make some new non-romantic friends.

Keep seeing people, but go very slowly this time.

Plunge witlessly into another nightmare.

Nothing will make your next Love Nightmare better than knowing it fills your former smoochy-woochy with anguish and rage.

Tips for
your next lifelong
relationship

➤ Don't worry if your new tickle bear is less attractive than your old kissy-wissy. An ugly tickle bear will bother kissy-wissy just as much.

➤ Make sure that your new relationship is one filled with honesty and openness. Except when it's easier to just lie about your past.

➤ And most important, realize that when you do find lifelong love, it probably won't be because you were looking for it. You'll probably just accidentally step in it.

Don't Repeat the Past!
Use these handy pages to keep notes
on old relationships that sucked!

⭐ (Shawna has a long one of these
placed in the corners of her brain)

Person's Name	Good Quality	Just some of the ways they suck

Person's Name	Good Quality	Just some of the ways they suck